BROOKLYN
The Centennial Edition

by BRIAN MERLIS

D1608994

Designed & Edited by Oscar Israelowitz

ISRAELOWITZ PUBLISHING

P.O.Box 228 Brooklyn, NY 11229
Tel. (718) 951-7072

Library of Congress Catalog Card Number: 97-72618
International Standard Book Number: 1-878741-33-0

Printed in Brooklyn, New York.

Cover Photo: *Franklin Avenue from Fulton Street (1910)*

Contents

Introduction

Brooklyn had its beginnings on June 16, 1636 with the first recorded land deed between the Dutch and the Canarsee Indians for a tract of property in what is now the Flatlands section. During its adolescence, Kings County consisted of six townships. By 1834, the Village of Brooklyn attained city status, and by 1896, all of the outlying townships of the county had been annexed by the sprawling City of Brooklyn. On January 1, 1898, by act of the State Legislature, the City of Brooklyn, which included all of Kings County, became a borough of the newly formed City of Greater New York.

1998 marks the centennial of this event. One can only contemplate whether the destiny of Brooklyn would have been different if it had retained its urban independence. This book attempts to capture, by way of some unique photographs, the authentic Brooklyn that many have come to revere, indeed to call *home*. A fascinating melange of ethnic groups, Brooklyn has come to symbolize a *melting pot*. Yet there is much more that suggests a love relationship with the past—a mind recollection of time and place interwoven with our nostalgic sense of cultural identity. Indeed, Brooklyn is more than just a place—it is a state of mind and a frame of reference.

From the outer reaches to its inner core, the name *Brooklyn* summons at once smiles of summers spent at Coney Island, sledding down hills at Prospect Park, taking in the beauty at the Botanical Gardens, enjoying a school trip to the Brooklyn Museum or rooting for *Dem Bums* at Ebbets Field. This is the Brooklyn millions remember, with its trolley cars, theaters, public schools, institutions and diverse places of worship. In toto, a mental picture post card of days long gone by but never to be forgotten. But above all, its will to survive the many vicissitudes of urban decay to be born once again—renewed both in the physical and the spiritual sense. This is evident by the recent reopening of Lundy's Restaurant as well as the enthusiastic efforts to return the Dodgers to Brooklyn.

Brooklyn holds a very special feeling by both its current residents and those who have since left. The borough's centennial should be a time to fondly recall its glorious past and to look ahead toward its next century with great anticipation.

Jack Merlis
Lee Rosenzweig

6

Acknowledgements

This book would not have been possible without the cooperation of many individuals. Thanks to Allen Kent and Bob and Helene Stonehill for allowing me to reproduce items from their collections. Photographs by Ron Zeil, William D. Slade, Max Hubacher, Sidney D. Silleck, Jr., Edward F. Watson, Herbert Budowle, Eugene Armbruster and Edward Rutter are featured in this edition. Dealers Nellie Huttunen, Helen DiMaria, Ron Marzlock, Charles Shapiro, Joel Streich, Joan Kay and Richard Selkowitz have all supplied images used in this volume. Louis Castaldo, Howard Rose, Lee Rosenzweig, Rita and Jack Merlis, I. Stephen Miller, and Ron Schweiger have all been so supportive of this project. Vincent F. Seyfried, my mentor, has set the high standards of writing which I hope one day to attain. My editors, Steve Brown and Kenny Kimmel helped to Anglicize my writing. Publisher Oscar Israelowitz, put the whole thing together so splendidly, as usual. Special thanks to family members Debbie, Heather and Josh for permitting me to pursue this time-consuming hobby.

Brian Merlis

Bath Beach

NOSTRAND HOMESTEAD - 1912
Looking from Cropsey Avenue *(Bath Beach)*
The Nostrand Homestead was located between Cropsey Avenue and Gravesend Bay, just east of 20th Avenue. The Nostrand family was one of the most prominent in New Utrecht and was involved in real estate. The Belt Parkway now runs through this waterfront property

BAY 28th Street - 1912
Looking from Benson Avenue to 86th Street *(Bath Beach)*
This part of Bath Beach still contains many Victorian homes, although some have recently been demolished or drastically remodeled. In this photo, children posing in the center of the tree-lined street convey a sense of living in a small town.

ENGINE COMPANY No. 143 - 1908
18th Avenue, looking northeast to 86th Street *(Bath Beach)*
This fire company celebrated its centennial anniversary in 1996.

HEGEMAN'S PHARMACY,
1746 CROPSEY AVENUE,
BATH BEACH.

HEGEMAN'S PHARMACY - 1910
No. 1746 Cropsey Avenue *(Bath Beach)*

Hegeman's Pharmacy, located on the corner of Bay 17th Street, filled prescriptions but also sold ice cream sodas and confections. Additionally, it served as a telegraph station and a meeting place for Bath Beach residents. This Mansard-roofed building has been gone for many years.

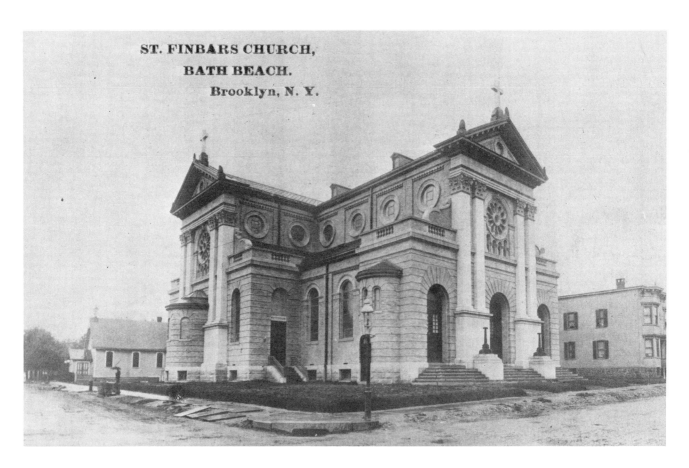

ST. FINBARS CHURCH,
BATH BEACH.
Brooklyn, N. Y.

SAINT FINBAR'S CHURCH - 1912
Benson Avenue & Bay 20th Street *(Bath Beach)*
Founded in 1881, Saint Finbar's is the most popular Roman Catholic Church in the Bath Beach section. This photo shows the newly constructed edifice and the older wooden church on Bay 20th Street, on the left.

84th St. Station, Bath Beach, Brooklyn, N. Y.

84th STREET RAILROAD STATION - 1912 *(Bath Beach)*
Prior to its elevation in 1916, the West End line to Coney Island ran at grade level. It skirted the lawn of the New Utrecht Dutch Reformed Church at 18th Avenue and then proceeded nearly parallel to 18th Avenue, behind the one-story brick building which today houses Maggio's Music Store. It then followed the route of the defunct Brooklyn, Greenwood & Bath Plank Road until it turned onto Bath Avenue and headed toward Coney Island. Trolleys later used the right-of-way.

Bay Ridge

BAY RIDGE WATERFRONT - 1898
Looking south from Bay Ridge Avenue *(Bay Ridge)*
This rustic scene, showing shacks surrounded by Ailanthus trees in the foreground, was recorded during the year in which Brooklyn became a borough of Greater New York City. Staten Island, across Upper New York Bay, is visible in the distance.

MANSIONS ALONG SHORE ROAD - 1908
Shore Road & 79th Street *(Bay Ridge)*
The Rulef Van Brunt house at right faced 80th Street. The Van Brunts were farmers who descended from the original Dutch settlers in the town of New Utrecht, which included Bay Ridge. The street lamps are along Shore Road. Both houses were razed prior to World War II.

THE CRESCENT ATHLETIC CLUB BOAT HOUSE - 1913 *(Bay Ridge)*
This imposing structure, located on the water at 83rd Street, was built for members of the elite Crescent Athletic Club.
It was destroyed by fire in the 1930s.

VILLAS OF BAY RIDGE - 1910
Shore Road, looking south from 99th Street *(Bay Ridge)*

Lillian Russell occupied the large villa on the left. It now houses a Catholic girls' school. At one time, Shore Road was where the rich and famous built their villas and mansions. They were attracted by the unobstructed view of the Upper New York Bay from the high bluff. Today, the Belt Parkway runs along the waterfront and almost all of these beautiful villas have been replaced by smaller homes and apartment buildings.

VILLAS OF BAY RIDGE - 1912
75th Street, looking east from Colonial Road *(Bay Ridge)*
This beautiful residential district is still one of Brooklyn's most desirable places to live. Ridge Boulevard is at the top of the hill.

HAMILTON HOUSE - 1961
Fourth Avenue at 101st Street *(Fort Hamilton)*
The Hamilton House was one of the area's most popular restaurants during the decades following World War II. An eatery bearing the same name and under the same management existed at this time on Ocean Avenue in Sheepshead Bay.

FIFTH AVENUE - ca. 1948
Looking northeast from Ovington Avenue *(Bay Ridge)*
The Loew's Alpine Theater is visible at Bay Ridge Avenue. Lyon's Stationary, on the corner, was there for decades.

**BAY RIDGE BRANCH -
BROOKLYN PUBLIC LIBRARY - 1912**
Second Avenue & 73rd Street *(Bay Ridge)*
In 1912, Elizabeth M. Skinner was librarian here.

STATEN ISLAND FERRY - 1964
69th Street entrance *(Bay Ridge)*
With the opening of the Verrazano-Narrows Bridge, the Staten Island Ferry - Brooklyn Branch, was soon discontinued. It ceased operation on Wednesday evening, November 25, 1964. The Belt Parkway is visible above the ferry entrance.

BELT PARKWAY - ca. 1960 *(Bay Ridge)*
An Oldsmobile passes a sign on which the Italian explorer's name is misspelled. A construction crane to the right of the sign, on the Staten Island side of the Narrows, is visible. The 13,700-foot suspension bridge, once the longest in the world, was designed by Othmar Ammann and was completed in 1964, a year ahead of schedule.

OUT FOR A SUNDAY DRIVE - ca. 1940

Bedford-Stuyvesant

THE LONDON HARNESS COMPANY - 1905
No. 1191 Bedford Avenue *(Bedford-Stuyvesant)*
Situated between Hancock and Jefferson Avenues, The London Harness Company supplied saddles, harnesses, whips and other equestrian accessories. As automobiles became more popular, businesses like this one ceased to exist.

BROOKLYN ORPHAN ASYLUM - 1910
Atlantic & Kingston Avenues *(Bedford-Stuyvesant)*
The Orphan Asylum Society of the City of Brooklyn, also known as the Beecher Home, was established in 1833. The massive structure was located on the northwest corner of Atlantic and Kingston Avenues. The institution could accommodate 300 orphans, ranging in age from three to thirteen.

PUBLIC SCHOOL - ca. 1915 *(Bedford-Stuyvesant)*
Portrait of Class 3-B.

ADVERTISEMENT, ca. 1908

ADVERTISEMENT, ca. 1930

ADVERTISEMENT, ca. 1915

FATHER & SON - ca. 1915 *(Bedford-Stuyvesant)*

Franklin Ave., from Fulton St., BROOKLYN, N.Y.

FRANKLIN AVENUE - 1910
Looking north from Fulton Street *(Bedford-Stuyvesant)*
The trolley is heading south to Coney Island. Elegant buildings with awnings and exquisite architectural details made Bedford-Stuyvesant one of the borough's most desirable places to live and was home to many of Brooklyn's most influential families.

ALTIERI'S SHOE REPAIR SHOP - ca. 1935
No. 144 Patchen Avenue *(Bedford-Stuyvesant)*
Shoemaker Pietro Altieri (left) is visited by his friend Carlo Rainone. The store was located on the west side of the avenue, between Putnam and Jefferson Avenues.

BLOCK PARTY - ca. 1900 *(Bedford-Stuyvesant)*
This traditional summertime event is still practiced throughout the borough. Note the hanging lanterns and American flags. It was probably the Fourth of July.

STREET SCENE - 1915
Monroe Street *(Bedford-Stuyvesant)*
Solidly constructed brownstones such as these on Monroe Street were built between 1880 and 1900. Attractive iron gates and railings enhance the overall appearance of these row houses.

THE BROOKLYN ICE PALACE - 1919
Atlantic Avenue near Bedford Avenue *(Bedford-Stuyvesant)*
The Brooklyn Ice Palace was located on the north side of Atlantic Avenue, where the road bends slightly, just east of Bedford Avenue. In addition to recreational skating, ice hockey matches were held there.

KIDS AT PLAY - 1960
No. 1281 Atlantic Avenue *(Bedford-Stuyvesant)*

FRANKLIN AVENUE - 1960
Looking north from Fulton to Hancock Streets *(Bedford-Stuyvesant)*
Problems of unemployment and alchoholism have always plagued Brooklyn's poor.
Racial prejudice is partly to blame for the slum conditions which many had to endure
then as well as now.

Bensonhurst

Bath Ave., Bensonhurst, N. Y.

BATH AVENUE - 1915
Looking northwest from Bay 31st Street *(Bensonhurst)*
The buildings in this photo still stand. The train has left Coney Island and will soon travel along New Utrecht Avenue and terminate at Second Avenue and 38th Street. A. Levinsohn's store is on the left. The area has been called "home" by immigrants of Italian and Jewish backgrounds since the turn of the century.

86th STREET - 1915
Looking northwest from 19th Avenue *(Bensonhurst)*
The theater at right offered "photo-plays" and silent movies. Within a year, the West End elevated would run above. This strip was immortalized sixty years later by John Travolta in the hit film *Saturday Night Fever.*

Borough Park

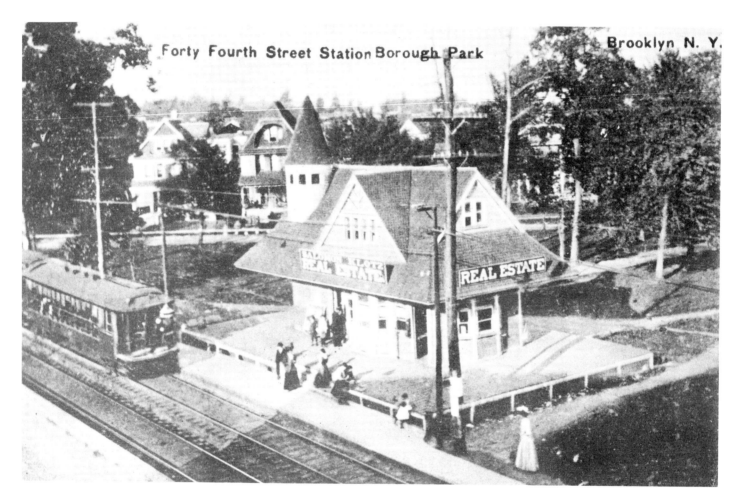

Forty Fourth Street Station Borough Park   Brooklyn N. Y.

REAL ESTATE

REAL ESTATE

44th STREET RAILROAD STATION - ca. 1912 *(Borough Park)*
The original West End line ran along New Utrecht Avenue on grade.

CORNERSTONE LAYING OF ISRAEL ZION HOSPITAL - June 29, 1919
10th Avenue at 48th Street *(Borough Park)*
On Sunday, June 29th, the community turned out for the laying of the cornerstone. It was a day of great fanfare. A marching band and automobiles led a grand parade through Borough Park, Bath Beach, Flatbush and Coney Island – the various communities the new hospital would serve. In 1943, Israel Zion merged with Beth Moses Hospital and became today's Maimonides Medical Center. *Courtesy of Maimonides Medical Center*

60th STREET - 1905
Looking southeast from the L.I.R.R. to 16th Avenue *(Borough Park)*
The first houses beyond 16th Avenue are No. 1617 on the left and No. 1618 on the right. The railroad grade crossing was eliminated about two years after this photo was taken.

NEW UTRECHT AVENUE - ca. 1912
North of 50th Street *(Borough Park)*

54th STREET - ca. 1912
Looking south from New Utrecht Avenue *(Borough Park)*

Brownsville

Hopkinson Theatre
HOPKINSON & PITKIN AVENUES   BROOKLYN, N. Y.

אַ פֿריילימער חלום

מיט זיסע, חאַרציגע נומערען געזאַנג, פֿון אייב שוואַרץ

נאָך דער פֿאָרשטעלונג אַ גרויסער אָל סטאַר קאָנצערט

מיט די גרעסטע סטאַרס פֿון דער אידישער בינע און ראַדיאָ

די גרעסטע ליבלינג	מנשה	יצחק	דזשוליוס
פֿון דער ראַדיאָ	סקולניק	פֿעלד	נאַטאַנזאָן
די אידישע מאַמע			
	סטאַר און דירעקטאָר	סטאַר און דירעקטאָר	סטאַר פֿון
אסתר פֿעלד	נעשאַנאַל טעאַטער 2טע עוו.	טעאַטער פּאַבליק טעאַטער	

טיקעטס שוין צו באַקומען אין באַקס אָפֿים פֿון טעאַטער

Wednesday Eve., November 16th
Testimonial for MR. OSCAR GREEN

MAX WILNER, HANNAH and ISIDOR HOLLANDER,
YACOB SUSSANOV and SIMON WOLF
In a New Musical Comedy

A HAPPY DREAM

Gala concert after the performance with Julius Nathanson,
Itzik Feld, Menasha Skulnik, Esther Field and others

YIDDISH THEATER PROGRAM - ca. 1935 *(Brownsville)*

LOEW'S PITKIN THEATER - ca. 1932
Pitkin Avenue at Barrett Street *(Brownsville)*
Brownsville's greatest movie house was designed with an ornate terra cotta façade by Thomas W. Lamb in 1931. The theater closed
in the 1970s but today houses a church.

BROOKLYN HEBREW HOME & HOSPITAL FOR THE AGED - 1920
Howard & Dumont Avenues *(Brownsville)*
Women light Sabbath candles (above) while the men pray in the synagogue (below).

Bushwick

BOHACK GROCERY STORE - ca. 1925 *(Bushwick)*
Founded in the late 1800s by Henry C. Bohack, the grocery grew into a large chain of stores. It became a forerunner of the modern supermarket, and lasted until the 1970s.

GREETINGS FROM HALSEY STREET - 1909
Halsey Street, looking north from Broadway *(Bushwick)*
Banners on the right advertise a laundry and a five and ten cent store.

GREENE AVENUE - 1911
Looking northeast toward Wyckoff Avenue *(Bushwick)*
The Long Island Railroad crosses Greene Avenue just beyond the attached frame houses on the right. The Brooklyn-Queens border crosses Greene Avenue three blocks north of this location.

Canarsie

CANARSIE ROAD - 1939
Rockaway Avenue (Canarsie Road) at Schenck Avenue *(Canarsie)*
The All American Hotel on the corner bears a banner displaying the Trylon and Perisphere, symbols of the 1939 World's Fair. The trolley is approaching Golden City Park, which was soon to be closed. The buildings in this photo are all gone.

GOLDEN CITY PARK - 1922 *(Canarsie)*
Golden City Park was located along the Canarsie shore. This newspaper advertisement shows the main entrance and the carousel building to the left. The amusement park opened on Memorial Day, 1907 and closed in 1939.

GOLDEN CITY PARK - 1919 *(Canarsie)*
New York's "Finest" patrolled all of Brooklyn's amusement areas. The ferris wheel is visible directly above the policeman.

SAVRAN'S SNACK BAR - 1950
No. 1070 Rockaway Avenue at Ditmas Avenue *(Canarsie)*
This restaurant served lunch to the workers at the nearby Canarsie Terminal Market which was recently built to replace the old Wallabout Market which was closed during World War II.

BETHELSHIP NORWEGIAN M.E.CHURCH - 1910
No. 297-299 Carroll Street *(Carroll Gardens)*
This church was organized in 1874. Located between Smith and Hoyt Streets, this church served Norwegian and Danish residents of the area.

Carroll Gardens

The Secretaries of the

CENTRAL BRANCH

Young Men's Christian Association

BROOKLYN, N.Y.

Wish you at this Season of Rejoicing

Much of the joy of living that comes from Physical Fitness;

Much of the satisfaction that results from an ever broadening Mental Vision;

and More and ever more of the abundance that enriches the life lived in the Spirit.

Christmas, 1912

BROWNSTONES - 1959 *(Clinton Hill)*
These homes were built in the 1880s as one-family residences. During the Great Depression many were converted into multi-family dwellings. The new apartments were rented to Blacks who fled the poor conditions of the South.

Clinton Hill

SNOWBALL FIGHT - 1960
Washington Avenue *(Clinton Hill)*
Brooklyn kids love a good snowball fight.

Coney Island

CONEY ISLAND - 1905
Looking east from the Centennial Tower (*Coney Island*)
Also known as the Observatory, this 300-foot tower was brought to Coney Island from the 1876 Philadelphia Centennial Exhibition. Seaside Park dominates the left foreground. Surf Avenue did not curve into Ocean Parkway at this time. The Brighton Beach Racetrack is at the left, just east of Ocean Parkway. The Hotel Brighton Beach, the Manhattan Beach Hotel and the Oriental Hotel are visible in the distance.

HOTEL BRIGHTON BEACH - 1915 *(Coney Island)*
Located just west of Coney Island Avenue, this luxurious hotel faced the ocean. It was designed by John G. Prague and was built in 1878. The hotel was demolished in 1923. To the far left, the Brighton Beach Music Hall is visible.

LUNA PARK - ca 1920 *(Coney Island)*
Among Luna Park's many attractions were the *Chutes*, the *Virginia Reel*, the *Trip to China* and the *Sheik's Harem*. Luna Park was the greatest amusement park of its day.

ENTRANCE TO LUNA PARK - 1911 *(Coney Island)*
Female ticket sellers are perched in ornate chariots. Arches supporting the grand Surf Avenue entrance
are overhead. Beyond the entrance are male ticket takers wearing Prussian-style pointed *(spitz)* helmets.

CIRCUS AT LUNA PARK - 1942 *(Coney Island)*
Luna Park boasted an eight-act circus as recently as the 1940s. As the years went by it became more difficult for
clowns, musicians and other entertainers to find work in Coney Island. Later that decade, Luna Park was destroyed
by fire.

STEEPLECHASE PARK - 1949
Surf Avenue at West 16th Street *(Coney Island)*
George C. Tilyou's famous amusement park existed from 1897 until 1965. The Parachute Jump ride was brought from Flushing, Queens, after the 1939 World's Fair closed in 1940. The abandoned Parachute Jump is still standing and has been called Brooklyn's Eiffel Tower.

TWO WOMEN ON THE BOARDWALK - ca. 1930 *(Coney Island)*
These two women are posing on the Steeplechase Pier. The boardwalk, completed in 1923, still attracts
 thousands of people throughout the year.

LIFEGUARDS AT CONEY ISLAND - 1920
Not exactly *Baywatch!*

RAVENHALLS BATHING BEACH - 1915
Foot of West 19th Street *(Coney Island)*
Before the Coney Island boardwalk opened in 1923, hotels such as Ravenhalls gave their patrons access to the beach. Bathers watch the steamboat *Howard Carroll* in the distance.

CONEY ISLAND - 1914
Surf Avenue, looking east from West 17th Street *(Coney Island)*
This was Coney Island during its heyday. Steeplechase Park is on the right and the towers at Luna Park's entrance are at the upper left. The Giant Racer rollercoaster, where today's Cyclone is, can be seen to the right of Henderson's sign.

NATHAN'S FAMOUS - 1942
Surf Avenue *(Coney Island)*
Founded in 1916, Nathan's quickly became a gastronomic institution. In this photo, the restaurant occupied only the building at Schweickerts Walk, but shortly afterward it expanded to Stillwell Avenue.

Crown Heights

BROOKLYN HOME FOR CONSUMPTIVES - 1910
No. 240 Kingston Avenue *(Crown Heights)*
This infirmary occupied half of a city block, on the west side of Kingston Avenue, between Sterling and St. Johns Places. It was organized in 1881.

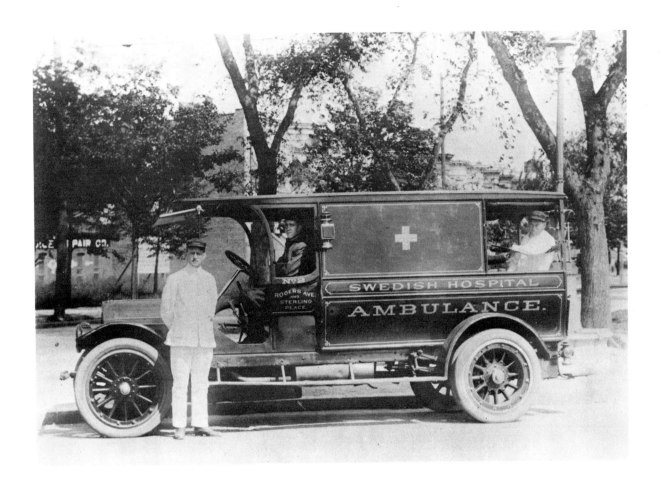

SWEDISH HOSPITAL AMBULANCE - ca. 1925 *(Crown Heights)*
Ambulance attendants and the driver pose on Eastern Parkway. The hospital, located at Rogers Avenue at Sterling Place, was where injured baseball players would be taken from Ebbets Field.

BERGEN STREET TROLLEY-BUS - 1960 *(Crown Heights)*
The trolley-bus served as a transition from the trolley to the bus. The view is looking east from Franklin Avenue.

A RIDE IN THE SUBWAY - 1949 (Opposite)
This IRT train originated from its Utica Avenue and Eastern Parkway terminus,
proceeded under Lexington Avenue in Manhattan, and terminated at Woodlawn in the Bronx.

Downtown

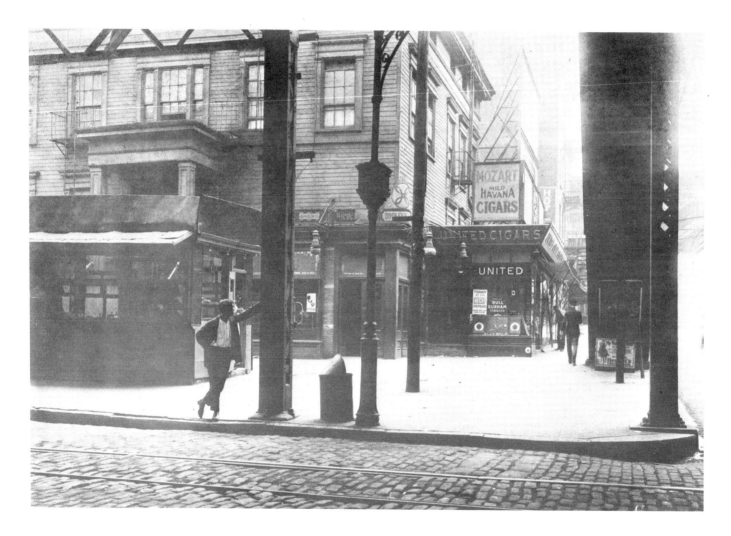

WASHINGTON & SANDS STREETS - ca. 1918
View of southeast corner *(Downtown)*
The Samuel Bowne House was built around 1840. It stood directly opposite the Brooklyn Bridge terminus. Its address was No. 145 Washington Street. A view of that side of the building can be found on page 76 of *Welcome Back to Brooklyn*.

DOWNTOWN BROOKLYN - 1954
Looking north on Court, Fulton & Washington Streets
From the steps of Borough Hall, the statue of Henry Ward Beecher aligns with the Brooklyn tower of the Manhattan Bridge. All buildings in this photo south of the Main Post Office Building would soon be razed for the construction of Cadman Plaza. The Mechanic's Bank Building on the left, and the Brooklyn Daily Eagle Building with the cupola, on the right, were the largest buildings to be demolished.

FIRE IN BROOKLYN - 1916
Flatbush Avenue, looking north at Livingston Street *(Downtown)*
A fire rages out of control near the Brooklyn Furniture Company, two blocks north
on Fulton Street. The Fifth Avenue elevated ran along Flatbush Avenue, from
Fulton Street to Fifth Avenue. Livingston Street is at left.

FIRE DEPARTMENT OFFICIALS - ca. 1920
No. 365-367 Jay Street *(Downtown)*
New York's "Bravest" pose in front of the Fire Department Headquarters. The 1892 Romanesque-Revival landmark building was designed by Frank Freeman. The curved lines on the lower left of the photo are cracks from the original eight by ten inch glass negative.

BROOKLYN PARAMOUNT THEATER - 1952
Flatbush & DeKalb Avenues *(Downtown)*
This great showplace would soon be the venue of Murray the K's historic Rock 'n' Roll productions.
After its 1962 closing, the theater became part of Long Island University's Brooklyn campus. It was
purchased by the school in 1950 and was rented to Paramount for an additional twelve years.

BLIZZARD ON FLATBUSH AVENUE - 1954 *(Downtown)*
The bus is traveling along Fulton Street. The marquee of the Fox Theater is on
the far left. The Paramount Theater is two blocks down, on the right.

ABRAHAM & STRAUS DEPARTMENT STORE - 1940
Fulton Street *(Downtown)*
The old and the new ways of delivering goods from Abraham & Straus to its thousands of Brooklyn customers.

ABRAHAM & STRAUS DEPARTMENT STORE - 1940
Fulton Street *(Downtown)*
Main entrance to the 1929 Art Deco Abraham & Straus Department store on Fulton Street.

ABRAHAM & STRAUS DEPARTMENT STORE - ca. 1948
Fulton Street *(Downtown)*
Employees' cafeteria on the roof of Abraham & Straus.

ABRAHAM & STRAUS DEPARTMENT STORE - 1940
Fulton Street *(Downtown)*
75th Anniversary Sale (1865-1940) in A & S' Basement.

SWEDISH PILGRIM CHURCH - 1941
413-415 Atlantic Avenue, looking east from Bond Street *(Downtown)*
The Swedish Pilgrim Church is located next to the Home of Ex-Lax. The brown-colored former factory was converted into condominiums. Just above the old Ex-Lax factory you can see the top of Brooklyn's tallest skyscraper, the Williamsburgh Savings Bank at Flatbush Avenue.

East New York

LIBERTY AVENUE - 1906
Looking east at Van Siclen Avenue *(East New York)*
Three modes of transport are documented in this photo, the elevated railroad, the trolley and the horse-drawn wagon.

PITKIN AVENUE - 1940
Nos. 2766 & 2768 Pitkin Avenue at Crescent Street *(East New York)*
Freedman's Luncheonette and the Crescent Kosher Deli occupied these two stores. This style of construction was popular during the building boom of the 1920s.

L. BARANOFSKY'S BAKERY - 1920s
Southwest corner Sutter & Snediker Avenues *(East New York)*
Behind the barber pole a sign advertises "Printing" in both English and Yiddish. Abraham Lesser's Radio Shop is highlighted on the billboard at left. His establishment was located at No. 631 Sutter Avenue, near Pennsylvania Avenue. His son David is a retired dentist living in Boca Raton, Florida. Brownsville begins immediately beyond the elevated Canarsie line.

KIDS WITH KNICKERS - 1910 *(East New York)*
Brooklyn street kids would often congregate near construction sites. Here, a group of boys pose beside a railroad embankment project.

Flatbush

THE MIDWOOD CLUB - 1905
East 21st Street, near Caton Avenue *(Flatbush)*
This Classic-Revival structure was built as the residence of David Clarkson, one of the wealthiest men in Flatbush. The Midwood Club, founded in 1889, moved into this building around 1900. It occupied nearly three acres on the west side of East 21st Street, 200 feet south of Caton Avenue. It was demolished in the 1930s. Apartment buildings were erected on its remaining half-acre property.

BEVERLY SQUARE EAST - 1901
East 19th Street, between Beverly & Cortelyou Roads *(Flatbush)*
This section of Victorian Flatbush was named *Beverly Square East* and was built up by T.B. Ackerson. His nephew, Henry Ward Ackerson, is in his nineties. He still runs a real estate company in Brightwaters, Long Island, and sells the large homes which his uncle had built around 1910.

A. LIPPOLD

OCEAN AVENUE - 1905
Looking north from Newkirk Avenue *(Flatbush)*

These two large homes in the Ditmas Park section of Flatbush were constructed in 1899. The corner home on the left later became a synagogue, the Community Temple Beth Ohr. That Reform congregation recently merged with Temple Beth Emeth which is located on Church Avenue at Marlborough Road. The building is now used as a medical clinic.

THE ALBEMARLE THEATER - 1950s
Flatbush Avenue, looking south from Albemarle Road *(Flatbush)*
Macy's is visible on the corner of Tilden Avenue. Further down the street is Loew's Kings Theater. These ornate theaters were used for graduation exercises during the month of June.

GIRLS' BASKETBALL TEAM - ERASMUS HALL HIGH SCHOOL - 1901 (Opposite)
Flatbush Avenue, near Church Avenue *(Flatbush)*
Interscholastic sports have had a long and glorious tradition throughout the borough. Propriety of the day dictated the wearing of cumbersome uniforms. Sneakers were not yet available at this time. Don't expect any slam dunks from this group!

EBBETS FIELD - April, 1960 *(Flatbush)*
The greatest loss to Brooklynites was the departure of their team, the Brooklyn Dodgers,
and the subsequent demolition of their stadium. The work was done by the firm of Harry Avirom.

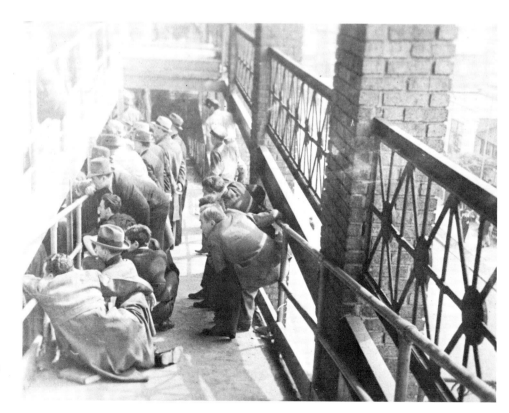

EBBETS FIELD - 1938 *(Flatbush)*
Fans watch a Dodger-Giant game from
he upper-level ramp.

EBBETS FIELD - 1957 *(Flatbush)*
This photo shows a wonderful bird's-eye view of the great ballpark.

PIGTOWN - 1936
Empire Boulevard & Nostrand Avenue *(Flatbush)*
Trolley wires form a web near a branch of the Bank of Manhattan Company. A man wearing an undershirt leans on a mailbox and reads a newspaper. This section of Flatbush was affectionately known as *Pigtown*.

CHURCH AVENUE - 1953
Between Ocean Avenue & East 19th Street *(Flatbush)*
Various stores, including the Turkey Bar, line the south side of Church Avenue. The apartment house was built in the 1920s on the former site of three Victorian homes.

Flatlands

STREET SCENE - 1946
Flatbush & Flatlands Avenue *(Flatlands)*
The photographer stood at the corner of St. Thomas Aquinas Church, which was founded in 1883. The buildings with the Flemish gables were built in 1926, possibly to commemorate the 300th anniversary of the Dutch settlement of Flatlands in 1636. The building on the northeast corner still houses a bank. Mac's Men's Shop is still next to the bank. The apartment house on the left edge of the photo collapsed in the summer of 1997.

RESIDENTIAL DEVELOPMENT - ca. 1939
Avenue H, in the East 40s *(Flatlands)*
These small brick attached homes were built by Roche and sold for the modest sum of $4,990.

Fort Greene

ADELPHI COLLEGE GYMNASIUM - 1908
Lafayette Avenue & St. James Place *(Fort Greene)*

Adelphi Academy was founded by John Lockwood in a home at No. 336 Adelphi Street in September, 1863. The all-boys school was so successful that a new building was erected with the Reverend Henry Ward Beecher laying the cornerstone on July 23, 1867. During the 1870s and 1880s additional wings were added with the financial support of Charles Pratt and others. The Clifton Place building was opened in 1889 but was nearly destroyed by fire that same year. By 1891, over 1000 students were enrolled. In 1896, Adelphi College was incorporated, offering co-educational courses of study. The Reverend S. Parkes Cadman was president of Adelphi College in the 1910s.

Gravesend

TROUBLE ON THE TROLLEY - 1906
Gravesend Avenue, looking north of Gravesend Neck Road *(Gravesend)*
This photo was taken after the Brooklyn Rapid Transit Co. raised its fare. Converging trolleys from various street lines were unable to proceed as a scuffle broke out on the cars. The photographer was positioned on the second floor of No. 2338 Gravesend (McDonald) Avenue, on the southwest corner of Gravesend Neck Road. The large building with the Mansard roof is just south of Village Road North.

CHILDREN AT PLAY - 1915
West 2nd Street, looking north to Avenue P *(Gravesend)*
This section was known as Marlboro. The children are playing in front of No. 1634 West 2nd Street. The rear of No. 279 Avenue P is clearly visible. Many of Brooklyn's southern sections retained their rural appearances until the building boom of the 1920s.

KINGS HIGHWAY - 1954
Looking east from McDonald Avenue (*Gravesend*)

This photo was taken from the F train elevated structure. The property on the south side of Kings Highway was part of the Gravesend Race Track. It was owned by the Brooklyn Jockey Club until the early 1920s, when it was sold off as residential lots. Most of the buildings in this photo were constructed during the 1920s. The two old houses at the far left date back to the days when Gravesend was an autonomous township, prior to 1894.

SINGER'S MODEL IIOMES - 1908
West 8th Street, south of Kings Highway (*Gravesend*)

One could purchase a solid brick house in the beautiful Gravesend section in 1908 for as little as $4,500. These homes, and many others on West 9th and West 10th Streets, are still standing. Pictured are Nos. 1767 and 1769 West 8th Street, between Kings Highway and Highlawn Avenue.

Greenpoint

FAMILY PORTRAIT - 1908 *(Greenpoint)*
Mabel and her baby sister Dorothy pose with mother and grandmother in their Greenpoint kitchen behind the store at No. 209 Nassau Avenue. The photo dates from January 8, 1908.

MANHATTAN AVENUE - 1929
Looking north to Nassau Avenue *(Greenpoint)*
The Stock Market Crash of October, 1929 affected many Brooklynites. Unemployment and foreclosure were commonplace during the Great Depression which followed.

DELIVERY TRUCK - 1916 *(Greenpoint)*
The Long Island Soap Works, located at Meeker Avenue and Bridgewater Street, manufactured many products. Rex Automobile Soap was delivered throughout the borough in open-air trucks.

BROOME STREET - 1929
Looking east toward Humboldt Street *(Greenpoint)*
The store on the left was owned by Joseph Ginsburg. He sold candy, cigars and newspapers from
No. 598 Humboldt Street.

DITMAS APARTMENTS & THEATER - 1912
Northeast corner Gravesend (McDonald) & Ditmas Avenues *(Kensington)*
The Ditmas Theater featured "photo-plays" and Vaudeville shows until it closed in the 1920s. Louis Fenning's bar occupied the corner store. Today, the Ditmas Avenue station on the F train elevated casts a shadow upon most of this view.

GRAVESEND (McDONALD) AVENUE - 1912
Looking south from Ditmas Avenue *(Kensington)*
In 1912, the Culver line ran at grade (street level). The elevated was completed in 1917. The wood-frame building down the block was the Kensington Station of the Culver line. The Culver line was originally known as the Prospect Park & Coney Island Railroad and was constructed by Andrew Culver in the 1870s.

Kensington

POLICEMAN ON HORSE - 1909
Fort Hamilton Avenue, looking west from Ocean Parkway *(Kensington)*
A mounted police officer patrols the entrance to the road which stretches a distance of four miles -- from this point west to the U.S. Government reservation at the Narrows. The tower visible on the right, just before East 4th Street, belongs to the Immaculate Heart of Mary Roman Catholic Church, which was founded in 1893. It has since been replaced by its beautiful orange brick sanctuary. Just behind the trees on the left is Public School No. 130, which still faces Ocean Parkway and the Prospect Expressway. Fort Hamilton Avenue has been renamed Fort Hamilton Parkway.

Lefferts Park

STREET SCENE - 1924
No. 1567 73rd Street *(Lefferts Park)*
A young woman poses with one foot on the running board of a late-model automobile.

Mapleton Park

61st St. from 20th Ave., Brooklyn, N. Y.

61st STREET - 1915
Looking from 20th to 19th Avenues *(Mapleton Park)*
A milkman is making early-morning deliveries to these recently constructed row houses in Mapleton Park.

PUBLIC SCHOOL No. 152 - 1915
Glenwood Road & East 24th Street *(Midwood)*
Neighborhood kids play stickball and hopscotch in the school yard. Today, the school yard is used as a parking lot for teachers from this school as well as from Midwood High School, now located across Bedford Avenue.

EAST MIDWOOD
The Finest
Residential Park in Flatbush

Thousands of dollars have been spent in making this property the most beautiful residential section in Flatbush. East Midwood has every city convenience. At its door is the Brighton Beach "L," the best rapid transit line to Manhattan, with through express service to Park Row in 30 minutes; 15 minutes to the beaches.

Over 200 Corbin Houses are in course of construction in this beautiful residence park. Prices from $6,500 to $13,750. Small amount cash; balance in small monthly payments. Write to JOHN M. DEMAREST, Sales Manager, for Illustrated Booklet "L."
Largest Builders of Houses of Quality in the World

JOHN R. CORBIN CO. FLATBUSH— Foster Av. B'KLYN and
Take Brighton Beach "L" Train to Newkirk Ave. Station   Brighton Beach R. R.

Midwood

KINGS HIGHWAY STATION - 1912
Looking east from East 15th Street *(Midwood)*
A Trommer's Brewery wagon hitched to two horses is parked in front of No. 1502 Kings Highway. The Kings Highway Branch of the Brooklyn Public Library was housed in a small building adjacent to the elevated Brighton line. The Brighton line ran at grade (street level) until 1907.

KINGS OAKS - ca. 1910
East 21st Street, looking north from Kings Highway *(Midwood)*
This section of East 21st Street was also called Kenmore Place and was subdivided by Wood, Harmon & Co. as part of the Kings Oaks Development. The street had not yet been cut through to Avenue O, where the woods of the Hitching Estate are visible. These homes were built by Deed Realty Co.

CONEY ISLAND AVENUE - 1926
At Avenue L, northwest corner *(Midwood)*
Only two of these five newly built storefronts have been rented. Large trees
on vacant lots were common along Coney Island Avenue at this time,
as the area was originally wooded. These buildings are still standing.

OCEAN AVENUE - ca. 1915
Looking north to Avenue O, west side of street *(Midwood)*
The Ocean Avenue Garage was located at Nos. 2042-2044 Ocean Avenue. It was built around 1911 and demolished in the mid-1980s.
A medical services building was later built on the 40 x 150 foot lot. Houses on East 19th Street are visible on the left.

Park Slope

PROSPECT PARK - 1935
Ninth Street Entrance *(Park Slope)*
The Marquis de Lafayette played a major role during the American Revolution.
This bronze memorial plaque was erected and presented to Prospect Park on
May 10, 1917 by Henry Harteau, a Brooklynite of French descent. Its base served as a
convenient resting place for children.

GRAND ARMY PLAZA - 1947 *(Park Slope)* **(Opposite)**
The first interfaith Flag Day took place in June, 1947. Junior Naval Cadets march in the shadow of the Soldiers and Sailors Monument.
In attendance was Mayor William O'Dwyer. According to the Commander of the Cadets, "This parade was designed to lessen the power
of Communism and kindred anti-American propaganda." This event was an attempt to replace pre-war patriotic May Day parades.

FIFTH AVENUE - 1908
Looking northeast from 10th Street *(Park Slope)*
This shopping area was developed in the mid-1800s. John McCormick's Dry Goods Store was located at No. 556 Fifth Avenue, and is visible at left.

PUBLIC SCHOOL No. 39 - 1908
Sixth Avenue & 8th Street *(Park Slope)*
This old school building is still being used. When this photo was taken, Mary Swyny was principal and in charge of nearly 1200 children utilizing 27 classrooms.

RALLY AT PROSPECT PARK - 1967
Grand Army Plaza *(Park Slope)*
On April 9, 1967 Mayor John V. Lindsay rides with several local children to "Keep the Prospect Park Boathouse." The Madonna Residence building is on the right.

WOMAN WITH FLAG - 1918 *(Park Slope)*
The image of another flag is visible between the fibers of the flag in the foreground.

I'VE BEEN WORKING ON THE RAILROAD - ca. 1919
Laborers of all backgrounds and nationalities risked their lives to construct the largest
subway system in the world. The workers are seen here taking a break.

PROSPECT HALL - 1908
Prospect Avenue, looking northwest toward Fifth Avenue *(Park Slope)*
Since 1959, the Prospect Expressway has run along the west side of Prospect Avenue. Although all of the buildings on
the left side of this photo are gone, several structures on the right side of Prospect Avenue have survived, including
Prospect Hall, seen behind the tree. The Fifth Avenue elevated, seen crossing over Prospect Avenue, has also been
demolished.

Parkville

CYCLE PATH ALONG OCEAN PARKWAY - 1912
Looking south from Lawrence Avenue *(Parkville)*
Parkville was developed in the 1850s, about twenty years prior to the construction of Ocean Parkway. This path is still used by cyclists as well as walkers and joggers. Equestrians still use the path across the parkway. The Mansard-roofed building on the corner housed a drug store.

Prospect Heights

Brooklyn Home for Aged Men, Classon Avenue.   BROOKLYN, N. Y.

BROOKLYN HOME FOR AGED MEN - 1915
No. 745 Classon Avenue *(Prospect Heights)*
Established in 1878, the Brooklyn Home for Aged Men was located on Classon Avenue, between Prospect and Park Places.

GRAND AVENUE - 1960
Looking north from Prospect Place *(Prospect Heights)*
The old-fashioned street lamp and street sign have all been replaced with
modern high-intensity street fixtures.

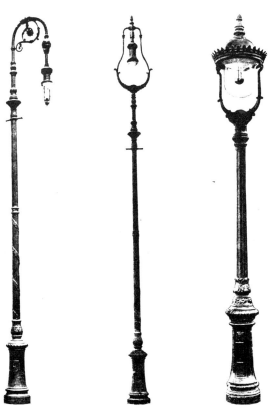

TYPICAL BROOKLYN STREET LAMPS

Sheepshead Bay

WINTER SCENE - ca. 1940 *(Sheepshead Bay)*
A frozen Sheepshead Bay was photographed from the apartment building along Shore Boulevard. The Bay View apartments is on the left. The Marine Parkway Bridge to the Rockaways is faintly visible toward the right, along the horizon. The small park in the foreground has recently been dedicated as the Holocaust Memorial.

F.W.I.L. LUNDY BROS. RESTAURANT - 1951
Emmons & Ocean Avenue *(Sheepshead Bay)*
The Lundy family was in the wholesale fish business since the late 1800s. The landmark building was built in 1934. Lundy's was closed from 1979 until it was re-opened by the Cretella family in 1995. The tradition lives on. This photo was taken on the last day of operation of the Ocean Avenue trolley.

EMMONS AVENUE - 1935
Looking west from Ocean Avenue *(Sheepshead Bay)*
A trolley bound for Sea Gate passes the recently built Lundy's Restaurant. Construction equipment on the left of the trolley was used to widen Emmons Avenue by 40 feet and build bulkheads along Sheepshead Bay. The Bay View Apartments are visible at Sheepshead Bay Road.

South Brooklyn

NORWEGIAN LUTHERAN DEACONESSES'
HOME & HOSPITAL AMBULANCE - 1910 *(South Brooklyn)*
This horse-drawn ambulance transported the injured and infirm. The Norwegian Lutheran Deaconesses' Home and Hospital, located at Fourth Avenue at 46th Street, was established in 1883. It cared for all persons, except those with contagious diseases. The hospital offered its services at no charge to the poor.

FIFTH AVENUE - 1908
Looking northeast at 52nd Street *(South Brooklyn)*
This neighborhood is today called Sunset Park. Fifth Avenue is one of Brooklyn's longest commercial strips, extending from Atlantic Avenue to the Fort Hamilton section.

GOWANUS EXPRESSWAY UNDER CONSTRUCTION - 1941
Third Avenue *(South Brooklyn)*
Hundreds of buildings on the east side of Third Avenue were demolished during the construction of this major Brooklyn highway. The steel was supplied by Harris Structural Steel Company. In 1998, the Gowanus Expressway is still under construction!

SUNSET PARK - 1908 *(South Brooklyn)*
This 25-acre park rises to a height of 163 feet above sea level. Its scenic lake was
later replaced by a swimming pool.

PUBLIC SCHOOL No. 136 - 1911
Fourth Avenue & 41st Street *(South Brooklyn)*
This large building exemplified the new style in public school design. It was built in the early 1900s.
C.O. Dewey was principal of Public School No. 136. Student enrollment in 1911 was 1,745.

Wallabout

BROOKLYN NAVY YARD - 1940

Sands Street Entrance *(Wallabout)*

By 1940, America began gearing up for war. To prepare our defenses, the Navy Department mandated that 11,000 workers begin recon-ditioning its aging fleet. The *U.S.S. North Carolina,* a 35,000-ton battleship completed at the Brooklyn Navy Yard, was the first to be built there since 1921. This photo shows a small group of workers leaving the facility after working the day shift.

Williamsburg

CONGREGATION KETHER TORAH - ca. 1925
159 Throop Avenue *(Williamsburg)*
This view of the northeast corner of Throop Avenue and Ellery Street is today the site of the Woodhull Medical and Mental Center.

PORTRAIT - ca. 1910 *(Williamsburg)*
This photo of Annie Loe Lake was taken in the backyard of
Dr. John Clayland who lived at No. 150 Hewes Street. The water
tower in the background is atop No. 151 Lee Avenue.

"CHEAP" ABRAMS - 1921 (Opposite)
No. 27 Whipple Street *(Williamsburg)*
The fence at right surrounded Public School No. 168, which faced Throop Avenue. Abrams' Candy Store was on the west side of Whipple Street, which runs for only two blocks, from Broadway to Flushing Avenue. This location is a block from All Saints R.C. Church and Pfizer & Co. Chemical Works.

CATALOG

BROOKLYN - THE CENTENNIAL EDITION
by Brian Merlis 132 pages   ISBN 1-878741-33-0 **$19.95** (plus $2.50 shipping)

WELCOME BACK TO BROOKLYN
by Brian Merlis & Oscar Israelowitz 172 pages   ISBN 1-878741-14-4 **$19.95** (plus $2.50 shipping)

BROOKLYN - THE WAY IT WAS
by Brian Merlis 250 pages (paper) ISBN 1-878741-09-8 **$24.95** (plus $2.50 shipping)
                             (hard cover) ISBN 1-878741-21-7 **$39.95** (plus $3.50 shipping)

BROOKLYN'S GOLD COAST - The Sheepshead Bay Communities
by Brian Merlis 160 pages (paper) ISBN 1-878741-49-7 **$19.95** (plus $2.50 shipping)
                            (hard cover) ISBN 1-878741-48-9 **$24.95** (plus $3.00 shipping)

EARLY VIEWS OF BOROUGH PARK
by Oscar Israelowitz 95 pages   ISBN 1-878741-12-8 **$4.95** (plus $2.00 shipping)

FLATBUSH GUIDE
by Oscar Israelowitz 126 pages   ISBN 0-9611036-9-8 **$4.95** (plus $2.00 shipping)

CATSKILLS GUIDE
by Oscar Israelowitz 126 pages   ISBN 1-878741-07-1 **$4.95** (plus $2.00 shipping)

LOWER EAST SIDE TOURBOOK (4th Edition)
by Oscar Israelowitz 150 pages   ISBN 1-878741-24-1 **$9.95** (plus $2.00 shipping)

U.S. HOLOCAUST MEMORIAL MUSEUM & WASHINGTON, D.C. GUIDE
by Oscar Israelowitz 126 pages   ISBN 1-878741-16-0 **$7.95** (plus $2.00 shipping)

NEW YORK CITY SUBWAY GUIDE
by Oscar Israelowitz 260 pages   ISBN 0-961103607-1 **$6.95** (plus $2.50 shipping)

EAT YOUR WAY THROUGH AMERICA - A Kosher Dining Guide (4th Edition)
by Oscar Israelowitz 125 pages   ISBN 1-878741-32-2 **$6.95** (plus $1.75 shipping)

NEW YORK CITY JEWISH TRAVEL GUIDE (5th Edition)
by Oscar Israelowitz 196 pages   ISBN 1-878741-17-9 **$11.95** (plus $2.00 shipping)

UNITED STATES JEWISH TRAVEL GUIDE (4th Edition)
by Oscar Israelowitz 460 pages ISBN 1-878741-31-4 **$19.95** (plus $3.00 shipping)

GUIDE TO THE JEWISH WEST
by Oscar Israelowitz 320 pages   ISBN 1-878741-06-3 **$11.95** (plus $2.00 shipping)

EAT YOUR WAY THROUGH NEW YORK - A Kosher Dining Guide
by Oscar Israelowitz 125 pages   ISBN 1-878741-34-9 **$9.95** (plus $2.00 shipping)

GUIDE TO JEWISH EUROPE - Western Europe 9th Edition
by Oscar Israelowitz 354 pages   ISBN 1-878741-19-5 **$14.95** (plus $2.50 shipping)

ITALY JEWISH TRAVEL GUIDE
by Annie Sacerdoti 242 pages ISBN 1-878741-15-2 **$14.95** (plus $2.50 shipping)

ISRAEL TRAVEL GUIDE
by Oscar Israelowitz 350 pages   ISBN 1-878741-26-8 **$19.95** (plus $2.50 shipping)

CANADA JEWISH TRAVEL GUIDE
by Oscar Israelowitz 196 pages   ISBN 1-878741-10-1 **$9.95** (plus $2.00 shipping)

SYNAGOGUES OF THE UNITED STATES
by Oscar Israelowitz 200 pages   (paper) ISBN 1-878741-09-8 **$24.95** (plus $2.50 shipping)
                                   (hard cover) ISBN 1-878741-11-X **$29.95** (plus $3.00 shipping)

ISRAELOWITZ PUBLISHING   P.O.BOX 228 BROOKLYN, NY 11229   TEL. (718) 951-7072

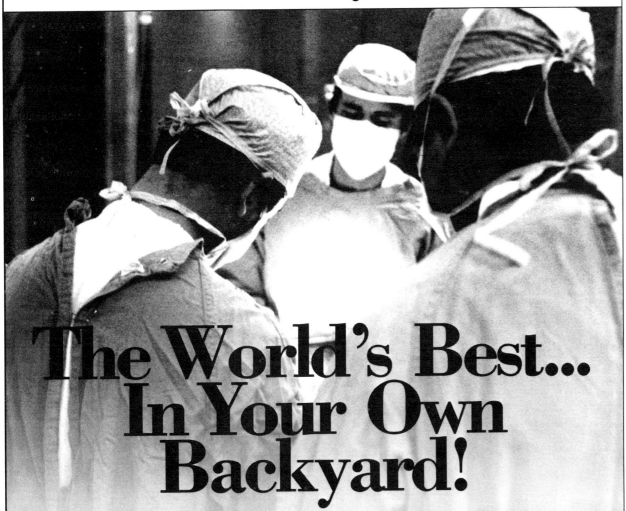

In Loving Memory of

GEORGE JOSEPH PHILIP MILLER

MARJORIE RUTH REISS MILLER

WHOSE PARENTS AND GRANDPARENTS SHAPED BROOKLYN

AS A GREAT BOROUGH OF NEW YORK CITY

Bessie Myers Reiss–daughter of Esther Devorah Lax Myers
and Jacob Urich Myers
Benjamin Reiss–son of Bessie Sturmlaufer Gottdank Reiss
and Louis Reiss
Celia Nirenberg Miller–daughter of Joan Nirenberg
and Jerome Nirenberg
Isidore Israel Miller–son of Rachel Miller and David Miller

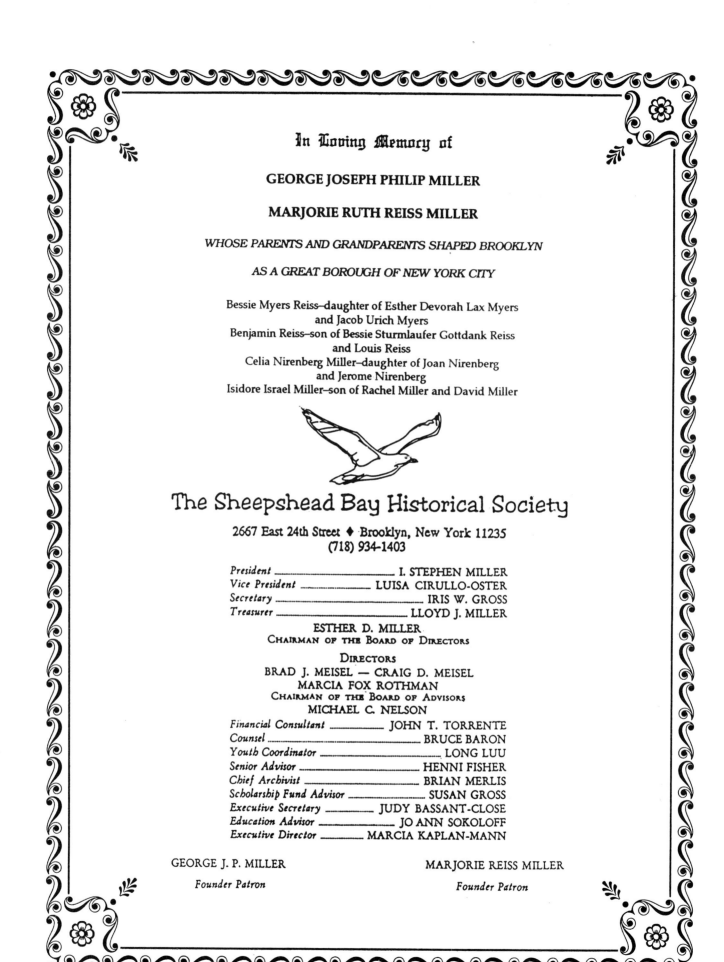

The Sheepshead Bay Historical Society

2667 East 24th Street ♦ Brooklyn, New York 11235
(718) 934-1403

President	I. STEPHEN MILLER
Vice President	LUISA CIRULLO-OSTER
Secretary	IRIS W. GROSS
Treasurer	LLOYD J. MILLER

ESTHER D. MILLER
CHAIRMAN OF THE BOARD OF DIRECTORS

DIRECTORS
BRAD J. MEISEL — CRAIG D. MEISEL
MARCIA FOX ROTHMAN
CHAIRMAN OF THE BOARD OF ADVISORS
MICHAEL C. NELSON

Financial Consultant	JOHN T. TORRENTE
Counsel	BRUCE BARON
Youth Coordinator	LONG LUU
Senior Advisor	HENNI FISHER
Chief Archivist	BRIAN MERLIS
Scholarship Fund Advisor	SUSAN GROSS
Executive Secretary	JUDY BASSANT-CLOSE
Education Advisor	JO ANN SOKOLOFF
Executive Director	MARCIA KAPLAN-MANN

GEORGE J. P. MILLER

Founder Patron

MARJORIE REISS MILLER

Founder Patron

Lundy Bros. Restaurant Salutes
Brian Merlis
for his Efforts in
Preserving Brooklyn's Heritage
for Generations to Come.